Management by Essay

Leading with Hope

Essays by Dave Bradley

Photographs by Tom Spitz

Kino Publishing

Management by Essay . . . Leading with Hope
Essays by Dave Bradley
Photographs by Tom Spitz

For further information, contact the author at:
Kino Publishing

TFG Press is a division of The Floating Gallery
244 Madison Avenue, #254
New York, NY 10016-2819
(877) 822-2500

Management by Essay . . . Leading with Hope
Essays by Dave Bradley
Photographs by Tom Spitz
1. Author 2. Title

Library of Congress Control Number   2003111986
ISBN 0-9745657-0-9

Printed in canada

This book is dedicated to the staff of La Paloma Family Services Inc., who have given of themselves for the last ten years in order to provide thousands of kids with the opportunity for a better life.

Table of Contents

Preface

Winter

Spring

Summer

Autumn

Introduction

Dave Bradley

*For Debbie, Brooke, Brian, Nathan and Sean,
my original inspirations.*

THESE WORDS ARE GREATLY ENHANCED by the artistry of my co-author Tom Spitz's photographic skills. I asked Tom to read each essay and produce a photograph that could serve as a symbolic representation of the words as he interpreted them. His talent is self evident.

This collection of essays was written by an executive director of a non-profit agency during a ten-year period. The pieces were distributed to staff and others through the agency's quarterly newsletter as well as in separate memos or letters on various occasions.

As a quarterly newsletter, nature's cadence, i.e., the season of the year, is inspiration for many of the pieces. The book is divided accordingly, although some of the

Author and his Father, 1960

essays do not necessarily have a seasonal theme. The introductions to each section will reveal my perennial mindset at that time of the year.

While a particular incident or encounter, including national tragedies, may have been the spark for some of the writings, the themes commented on have some permanency to them. Although the initial audience is the staff of a child welfare agency, the concepts of hope, resiliency and endurance, that are pervasive throughout these essays, can apply to nearly any work environment.

If I were to characterize these writings in one word, the concept of *hope* rises as the most salient theme that consistently occurs. In the practice of my profession, hope has always been a central concern. Helping people take effective control of their lives is predicated to a great degree on their ability and willingness to have enough hope to try. Hope has a duty to fill in the gaps left when faith and love falter. However, any profession that relies heavily on the creative energy and perseverance of its staff can see their work reflected in these essays.

Every essay contains a lesson. Sometimes the lesson is obvious, sometimes less so. Nevertheless, the intent was always to provide food for thought, with the hope that thought would then lead to action. The action is rarely proscribed and not even alluded to in some of the essays. The pieces, when they work, stimulate readers to take up a mission of their own design.

My hope for publishing these essays is that others may find them useful in meeting the challenges of their everyday work life. Managing people is really about managing many missions. Gradually, I discovered that this means building an organization by finding and nurturing individuals who can fulfill their personal missions in a community of common purpose. I found it helpful and rewarding to write to them. These are the letters I wrote to and for them.

Fall 2003

Introduction

Tom Spitz

For Jill, Angel, Eliot and Baxter, who with each new day,
encourage and inspire me.

LIFE IS A JOURNEY MARKED by triumphs and pitfalls. Sometimes we stumble, but we find a way to get back up and continue onward.

I've crossed paths with many on my photographic journey – people who have, in some way, left a lasting impression on me. Faces and memories I will carry with me always.

When Dave approached me about this book and asked me to share my work with him, I was honored. I was also inspired by the possibility to showcase those little moments in life that sometimes go unnoticed.

From the very first essay, I found in his words a sense of hope, a belief that real life – at its best and at its worst – offers so many lessons for all of us. By taking the time to ponder what is happening around us, we can learn much about running a business, managing people, and becoming the best people we can be.

From the very beginning of this project, I believed this would be a perfect marriage of his words and my photographs. I hope you think so, too.

Acknowledgements

AS WITH ANY UNDERTAKING SUCH as this, there are many people to thank. I am grateful to the following people for their contributions and assistance in producing this book: my wife Debbie D'Amore for her encouragement and support in completing this project; my son, Sean Bradley for formatting the text and pictures; my friend Carol Schaefer for editing each and every essay; my professional peers, Dan Ranieri and David Giles for their taking the time to read and recommend these essays; to my friend Janet Jung for the same.

I greatly appreciate Jose Galvez for his endorsement of our work. I would like to thank my coworkers at La Paloma Family Services, Inc. in Tucson, particularly, Debbie Hughes for publishing these essays in our quarterly newsletter and the rest of the staff who were often the source of inspiration for many of these essays.

I am extremely grateful to the many children that I have worked with over the last 20 plus years and whom I have written about in many of these essays. In many ways their life stories have become the part of me that I wanted to expose in this book.

In addition to Tom's artistic skills, I am very grateful for those many individuals whom he captured on film and who have become such an integral part of this book. My thanks to them for sharing their beauty and grace with us.

Winter

WINTER BRIDGES THE END OF one calendar year and the beginning of an-other. We usually find ourselves looking backward and forward at the same time. These essays focus on our resolve to build a better future by building on the best of the past.

Energy is required to carry on against the odds. **Who Will Stoke the Fire** is a brief reflection on the need to carry the torch through thick and thin.

Looking back on a year that contained the tragedy of September 11th, **An Image of Promise** focuses on interdependence and hope for a better world.

The concept of looking back, looking forward sets the stage for **In the Field, Harvesting Hope.** Destinies can be set in motion by the simple tipping of scales at an early age.

Time is Life makes it clear that we can measure the value of our lives by noticing what we are doing moment to moment.

Unexpectedly, we might be called upon to carry out a duty we did not initially consider. **Little Did We Know** highlights the cost of love.

Focusing on the best of our communal life is the best building block we have for the future. **The Continuation of Common Dreams** brings to mind the importance of focusing on the positive to build a better future.

Always be prepared to be startled into being reminded what is important when you least expect it. **Everyone's Child** illustrates our interconnectedness and duty to care for one another.

Ultimately, life begins and ends with love. **Come Home** calls us back to what we really value and how we must always work for it.

The millennium was a crossing over. **In the Dawn of Century 21** calls us to bring with us what we learned in the previous century on to the next century in order to make better the world.

We often don't stop and think about how much effect we have on other's lives. The power of memory gives us a lifetime commission. You should stop, pat yourself on the back and **Be Comforted by Your Good Works.**

Disappointment can become a catalyst for action and change just as much as it can destroy our hopes and aspirations. The final essay is a call to character.

Who will Stoke the Fire?

Some day, after we have mastered
the winds, the waves, the tides of gravity,
we will harness the energies of love
and then for the second time in the
history of the world, humankind
*will have discovered **fire**.*

—*Teilhard de Chardin*

FORTUNATELY, MOST OF US HAVE experienced the fire that the philosopher alludes to.

Ultimately, the children, for whom we work will need to be touched by the fire if they are to have any chance of success in life.

The fuel for love is the hope that we must offer our children. Though emotionally, physically, and psychologically battered, we must prove to them that they are not broken. Despite their best efforts to extinguish the flame, through running away or acting up, being belligerent and self destructive, we must keep their hope alive.

The temptation to surrender to despair, doubt, and sadness is always with us. The challenge of our work is to stoke the fire even when we are tired, frustrated, and angry.

For many of our children we are the first chance. For others, we are the last hope. If they are ever to experience even a spark of love, we may be their first opportunity.

It will always be true that you cannot give what you do not have. Our Agency is only as good as you are individually and we are collectively. Our children need our best from us.

I hope this season gives you a chance to renew your spirit, to rekindle your hope, and to increase the flame of love in your life.

WHO WILL STOKE THE FIRE?
Those whose great good fortune it is
to have their hearts touched by it.

An Image of Promise

"The world of nature is so small and interdependent that a butterfly
flapping its wings in the Amazon rainforest can generate a violent storm on
the other side of the earth.
This principle is known as the "Butterfly Effect."
Today we realize that the world of human activity has its own
"Butterfly Effect" – for better or worse."
—Kofi Annan, 2001 Nobel Peace Prize Address

IN A YEAR MADE HORRIFIC by exploding airplanes and crashing buildings, let us end it with an image of promise. Together, let's listen for the almost inaudible fluttering of a butterfly's wings. Though fragile, on these wings, rest our hope, our faith and our love. These are the immeasurable variables that change the lives of those we serve.

Chaos is not necessarily a bad thing. In fact in many scientific fields, as Mr. Annan alludes to above, chaos is now an accepted and central concept upon which the universe counts on to operate.

Chaos is stated in contrast to scientific determinism, which asserts that if I can accurately describe a condition and what forces are acting on that condition, I can predict the outcome of any future event. I can also explain the cause of past events using the same principle.

Determinism further presumes that we can measure exactly what conditions and forces are applied in any particular situation. However, no matter how sophisticated the measurement there is always a margin of error which produces results that could not be predicted.

This problem of measurement is called the Butterfly Effect. Because of our inability to measure all conditions all of the time with absolute accuracy, there is always a degree of inaccuracy in prediction. Importantly, the earlier in the process a measuring error occurs the bigger the unpredictability of the final result.

Translated to what we do, caring for young lives, the Butterfly Effect takes on even greater meaning. How connected we are! A slight intervention, a look, a touch, or a word has the power to alter the trajectory of a life. An act barely measurable because of its small size becomes, in the future, immeasurable in its enormity.

What science calls chaos we call hope, faith and love!

The lives of the kids we serve are not predetermined. This is true no matter how much violence they witness or suffer, how disturbed they may present to us, how far behind they are in school, or how difficult they maybe.

The Butterfly Effect gives us that spark of hope that there are aspects of our kids' lives we cannot measure, do not know and cannot predict. Most encouraging of all, this spark can portend a radiant life of new meaning and purpose.

Because the universe counts on this inevitability of chaos, we have no right to give up on another human being. Ironically, chaos as opposed to predictability is kindling for our faith that people can change. It fuels our hope that a better life is within reach and it is the fire of love we need to lead our kids to productive adulthood.

Until our final breath, we are each of us a work in progress, always building, dreaming, learning, changing and growing. Science tells us that when butterflies work in sufficient numbers they can literally move the heavens. Similarly, when we work together in common purpose we can move the worlds of the children we serve.

In the Field, Harvesting Hope

We will rest but not tarry.
For beyond our field children are waiting.
Their lives to be renewed,
their spirits to be nurtured,
their hopes to be harvested.

THE ROMANS NAMED THEIR FIRST month of the year after the two faced god, Janus. He is portrayed with one face looking back and the other forward. Janus seems an appropriate symbol for the anticipation that marks the second millennium's countdown, now only a few days away.

The end of any particular time frame always portends the beginning of another. The Latin words *respice* and *prospice* reflect the healthy notion of reflection and projection as the year, decade, century and millennium draw to a close.

Our morning paper last month brought to mind this notion of *respice* and *prospice* in very human terms. The simultaneous arrival of both good and bad news is always startling and disconcerting. One story told of self-discipline and reaching dreams the other of self-destruction and tragedy. Both stories, although opposite in the emotions evoked, are connected, as are all stories of kids who grow up in the 'system'.

Over breakfast, two destinies collided in separate sections of the daily paper. Their individual stories reveal a tale of crisscrossed lives. One looking forward to the bright stars, a *prospice*, a promising future, the other now trapped behind dark bars, a *respice*, looking back on unspeakable deeds.

Two of our kids, one present, one past made the news that day. Their backgrounds similar, their futures dramatically contrasted. Both young men were reared in adversity. Nevertheless, no one could have foretold their disparate fortunes.

Each caught the attention of others while performing in a field. One plays in a high school stadium under bright lights. His skill has transformed it into a field of dreams. One, in Cain like fashion, under the cover of night, transformed a plot of desert into a field of tragedy and nightmare. One pair of hands snatches a football from the sky, the other's fingers cradled a gun and a young girl died. In a uniform before large crowds one carries out the familiar rituals of sport, igniting cheers. The other is alone, vested, until his final days, in the drab orange of an accused murderer, inciting only fears.

Publicity usually is given to extremes. In these stories, one young man is breaking a sports record, the other has broken the most sacred of covenants, thou shall not kill. Their brief encounters with local fame and infamy may not linger long in the public eye. There will be other records and other murders.

Yet we who toil in this field and know both of these children cannot help but stop and take note. These 'breakings' that caught the media's attention don't tell the whole story of these two lives whose destinies meshed in a newspaper. The mysteries of nature and nurture are not easily solved. Both arrived in 'our field' with difficult histories. Efforts were made to save, protect, teach and nurture both. Is it simply that one learned and one did not? Did nature condemn one and save the other? Perhaps, but we cannot afford to reduce our efforts to change kids' lives and destines to simplistic or cynical explanations.

We too work in the field, our hands ceaselessly toiling. Our field is like a pasture where kids come from every type of background, bearing both good and bad seed. We *sow and care*, we *weed and encourage*, and we *reap and challenge*. Some of our kids grow and mature quickly, some move on to be nurtured by other hands, and some, as the parable goes, fall among the rocks out of reach.

While it would be more efficient if we could predict who would flourish in our field and respond to our efforts, may be we should be thankful that we can not easily foretell their destinies. We toil on through the day and night, with tools tempered in the fire of realism, but also hardened by a commitment to carry on no matter how tough the soil or how obdurate the plant.

In this time, a season of reflection and projection, we know this. When the demarcations of century and millennium pass by we will still be in the field. With satisfaction, we can look back knowing we have not toiled in vain. With anticipation, we will look forward to a world made better by our efforts.

Time is Life

Nothing that is worth doing can be achieved in a
lifetime; therefore, we must be saved by hope.
Nothing which is true or beautiful or good makes
complete sense in any immediate context of history;
therefore, we must be saved by faith.
Nothing we do, however virtuous,
can be accomplished alone.
Therefore, we are saved by love.

—Reinhold Niebuhr

A FEW BURNT ORANGE WESTERN skies from today and the morning light will belong to a new year. Our not too distant ancestors marked the passing of time in much broader terms than the movement of hands on a clock. The sun was only one of many celestial timepieces. Time was also calibrated by weather, crops, and nature's majestic and sometimes brutal staging of the cycle of life.

In a culture that emphasizes the correlation between time and money, we would do well to reflect on our foremothers and fathers penchant for measuring time in the context of their relationship with each other and their immediate environment. During this reflection perhaps we might rediscover that the past, present and future only have meaning in the context of these same relationships.

Stripped of all but the barest of necessities, our status in life can be reduced to our answers to one simple question, "Where are we in the context of our relationships with others?" This question, which life incessantly asks, demands not simply an answer but an affirmation.

As those who came before us realized long ago, our life is a journey whose value is rooted in the interdependence of family and friends. As we take time this holiday season to both reflect and project, let us affirm the relationships that are most important to us.

The coming year should prove to be an exciting period for our organization. It will only be so, however, if we are people who are bound together with the hope, faith, and love that Niebuhr refers to above. It is the practice of these essential virtues that brings <u>life</u> to the <u>time</u> we spend together.

As for the future, let us be guided by the confident and forward looking words of Walt Whitman, "Our best music has yet to be written, our finest songs have yet to be sung."

Little Did We Know

What I did not know, what I did not know
Of love's austere and lonely offices?

—**Robert Hayden**

HAYDEN'S WORDS ARE THE LAST two lines from a piece entitled, *Those Winter Sundays*. The poem recounts the author's realization, lamentably too late, of his father's daily sacrifices on his behalf for which Hayden never acknowledged or thanked him. *Love's austere and lonely offices* speaks to the duties that emanate from relationships; those acts of kindness, sometimes, heroism, that go unnoticed even in the closest, most significant and caring of relationships. It can also refer to those obligations, sometimes unexpected, or more accurately, unanticipated, that come to us as a function of our decision to work with people.

Recently, our staff carried out one of those 'austere and lonely offices' in the pews of a local funeral home attending a service for a former client of ours who took his own life just before the holidays. Statistically, the longer we do the type of work we do with the kids for whom we care, the probability increased that this day would come. Statistical probabilities offer no consolation when a lifeless young man is lying before you.

Carl Sandburg wrote, while observing people on the streets of Chicago caught in the hustle and bustle of life, that many of the passersby "seemed old before they were young." Lives being drained from people before 'youth' could even have its day. So it is when a life is cut short long before its prime. That the termination of that life was self-inflicted makes the draining of life even more stark. It is a heavy feeling that seems to age the mourners instantaneously. The hectic pace of our lives is always brought into question at such times. Death always asks of the living, what are you doing? What is important and why?

Rarely, wrote Hugh Prather, is suicide illogical, it is rather a misinterpretation of available information. It is an assessment made abruptly at times and pondered deeply at others, that a situation is hopeless, death the only recourse. Unfortunately, once played out, no reassessment can be made. The survivors assume this task.

We, who are left behind, inherit the austere duty of bringing purpose to this life, uncovering the spark of hope in the void of deep shadows. Better to light one candle than to curse the darkness, as the saying goes. It serves little purpose to dwell on the startling event that brought this life to a close. Our 'lonely office' is to keep the candle lit, even as the howl of despair blows by us. This abbreviated life had a purpose that we must now make manifest.

This was not a foreseen duty when he came to us as a young teen, troubled but full of life. But it is a duty that love and honor will not let us forsake. We are, perhaps unexpectedly, one with the poet. Little did we know of love's austere and lonely offices.

The Continuation Of Common Dreams

Many pictures of high endeavor...
Have been drawn for our use,
And bequeathed to us,
Not only for contemplation but for our emulation.

—Cicero

AS I REFLECT BACK OVER the last year many images come to mind. It seems important to recognize that we have the freedom to be selective about what we choose to recall from our shared experiences.

We hold in our memories a repository of countless encounters of the last twelve months. Many of those impressions will bring at least a smile, some a full-blown chuckle, while others may carry with them a degree of hurt, sorrow, or even offense.

Likewise, our kids carry with them memories of this time and their life among us. Our hope of changing their lives for the better is really contingent

upon their ability to reflect on, recall, and emulate that which we taught them, that is, that which we demonstrated by our words and actions. As we dealt with one another, they were on watch, learning from us.

Always then, let us keep in mind how indelible our actions, how powerful our influence and how significant our relationships with one another are on those whom we work with, as well as those we serve.

Let us agree to end the year in contemplation of the best of our common memories. Let us contract with one another to emulate our finest moments. Let us purge our hearts and minds of all that is negative. Let us build on the best of what we are and make the coming year a continuation of our common dreams.

Everyone's Child

It is only out of the future that the present can be lived
—Dietrich Bonhoeffer

BUSY, ON THE WAY TO an appointment, my attention is diverted while passing through a tree-laden square nestled among tall buildings. It is late afternoon in early November. There is a family resting against a cement planter. Fittingly, as the holidays approach, it is a very young mother and father with a baby. The child, not quite yet a toddler catches my attention first as his dad tosses him in the air, gently at first but more vigorously on my approach.

Seemingly suspended in mid air, wide eyed with arms grasping downward, his little body revolts in panic at this crude violation of gravity's demands. Burly tattooed arms provide the thrust for this momentary flight and young strong hands await the inevitable return.

The frightened airborne face does not look directly down but rather off to the side a bit. The look is one of supplication requesting a reprieve from this precarious exercise, being repeated now every few moments. Eighteen years old at most, the mother's instinctive response is to intervene and cease this torment. She advocates with a gentle touch to the muscled arm and a soft admonition, "you are scaring him." The intervention is rebuffed, rejected on the grounds that a lesson, presumably with much broader implications, is being taught. Fear is no excuse to interrupt this instruction. "This is good for him, it will make him tough and unafraid," says the self-assured voice, himself only a few years removed from childhood.

Our eyes meet, she and I. The mother and the child's advocate now assumes an added role, that of liaison with the outside world, the family's ambassador. This role, which has been thrust upon her unexpectedly, serves only to increase her level of discomfort.

My moving by quickly alleviates some of her stress, although our eyes connect and avert two more times. The looks contain a mixture of things, her palpable embarrassment over the behavior of her male companion, frustration at her inability to intervene successfully on behalf of her son, and a shrug of helplessness that may portend an ominous destiny for her young one.

Past them now, I look back a few times and wonder. Will her gentleness always be overruled? Will toughness be the measure of their child's manhood? Will the lessons in fearlessness always take precedence over those of wisdom and kindness? A decade or so hence will some future pastor, childcare worker or judge be looking into the face of a tough and fearless boy who averts his mother's eyes?

Perhaps, I am reading too much into a brief contact with a young family just beginning their life together. Against the odds, at least they are together and as time and circumstance mold their lives they may learn from one another. These arms that effortlessly toss the child into mid-air can be the same ones to hold and comfort him when first he scrapes his knee or encounters the neighborhood bully. And maybe that demure voice urging caution and gentleness will, in time, be transformed. One can imagine the infant as a man teaching his own son, "Nana taught me long ago that it is better to soothe fears than it is to create them."

The approaching season of hope encourages the foresight of a bright future for this child, a future full of opportunity and communal support. The truth is, we all, in one-way or another, have a stake in his destiny. Mother and father, who have much to learn, are the primary care takers, but all of us must be ready to answer the call as potential guides and guardians. In this sense, a child has been given unto all of us and none of us can afford to avert our eyes.

A nameless family in a city square beckons and reminds us of our duty to all children and one another. This seems very familiar… 'Tis the season.

Come Home

*"I will live in the Past, the Present, and the Future . . .
The Spirit of all three shall strive within me."*
—Ebenezer Scrooge
A Christmas Carol *by Charles Dickens*

NATURALLY, DURING THIS TIME OF year the book *A Christmas Carol* gets a lot of attention. There are numerous movies, plays, and even cartoon versions of the story of Ebenezer Scrooge's rehabilitation from the crusty quintessential skinflint to a generous and loving human being. This book on which all of these versions is based, is actually rather short and lends itself to a quick read. I would urge you to take the time to read it this holiday season.

It strikes me that the most compelling aspect of the three Spirits (Past, Present, Future), is that each Spirit calls upon Scrooge to *come home*. That is, to *come home* to what he **really** values. The Spirits essentially force Ebenezer to confront the reality that he needs to love, as well as be loved, despite his protestations that all of this nonsense is 'humbug.'

Eric Fromm, a psychiatrist and philosopher, noted in his book *The Art of Loving* that the difference between immature and mature love is this. "Immature love says that I love you because I need you. Mature love says I need you because I love you."

Ebenezer, in a very short period of time, transforms himself from an unloving and unlovable person to the mature lover that Fromm refers to. It is this transformation that makes the story so enduring, as well as, so 'unbelievable' particularly in this day and age. Nevertheless, the lesson of Scrooge's conversion can be learned and relearned by all of us.

The key elements of his transition are awareness, recollection, reconciliation, and choice. Ebenezer became acutely aware, with the help of the Spirits, from where he came. He recollects the importance of relationships, he reconciles with those whom he has offended, and he makes a deliberate choice to become a loving person, that is, a person who is, literally, in love with love.

This holiday season, my hope for all of us is that we can be renewed and reinvigorated by following Scrooge's path to mature love. Let's be aware of what we truly value, let's recollect how the important relationships in our lives shaped our perceptions. Let us reconcile, if necessary, with anybody that we have wronged, and come to realize that love is a decision.

In our work we are set apart from what the majority of people do for a living. We operate in a world that is foreign to many others. Our *'Spirits'* make unique demands upon us. Our kids demand much of our energy. At times, every step forward is paid for by a few steps backward. This condition will not change. We can, however, draw strength from our ability to stay focused on what we value, sustenance from holding to our mission, and energy by pursuing a life course that leads to the satisfaction and joy of mature love.

In the Dawn of Century 21

*This generation cannot afford to waste its
substance and its hope in the struggles of the past,
beyond these walls there are lives to be saved,
there is work to be done.*

—Robert Kennedy

IN WHAT MOST PEOPLE CONSIDER to be the last year of the decade, century, and millennium, the thrust is forward. The idea is that this coming year is the *last year* of these three significant time demarcations creates a certain degree of panic. While in some sense, it's just another year, it is special because we seem to be crossing over to something or somewhere we've never experienced or been before.

Just simple things, like writing a check that reads, January 1, 2000, seem eerie, as if the day were the dividing line between two distinct eras, one bygone, the other anticipated. Yet in a more mundane or practical sense it really is just another day. The same bills, struggles, joys, hopes, and fears that were with us on the day before will still be there on the first of January, Millennium three.

Despite that reality check, maybe it is a good thing for us to anticipate that day with some trepidation and excitement. Unlike other years, which expire with us holding resolutions that evaporate by February, maybe this can be a year of resolve that pushes us to prepare for the new century with increased vigor, purpose, and perseverance.

Think, for a moment, what the crossover to the next millennium holds for the children we serve. Will they harbor the same anticipation as we do, or will this event hold nothing for their imaginations? Will the struggles of the past keep them bound to the then bygone era, or will they break free to a newer world that holds hope and opportunity?

We stand on the precipice of a new era and there is work to be done. Many people will look back on those of us who crossed over to the new millennium to listen to what we were saying, to see what we were doing. They will evaluate us by the standard under which all civilizations are measured, "What did these people do to ensure that the weakest of them survived?" "What did they do for the children in their care, especially those disaffected, disconnected, and discarded from society?"

We, who do this business of caring for children, must be prepared to answer back to those who ask. We were there with these children. We were building relationships, we were enhancing their skills, we were fostering their sense of worth, and we were embracing the belief in each child's individual potential. We were there preparing them for the new era, hand in hand we crossed over with them, and challenged them to take control of their lives.

Let it be said of us that we diligently spent the last year of this millennium in service to the next generation. We worked hard in the words of John Paul II, "in order that their tears, spent in this century, would bring forth a bountiful harvest for them and their children in the dawn of century twenty-one."

Be Comforted by Your Good Works

*"My imagination, my love and reverence and admiration,
my sense of the miraculous is not so excited
by any event as by the remembrance of my youth."*
—**Henry David Thoreau**

Many of the voices our children bring with them when they arrive in our care neither comfort nor inspire them as they are confronted by life's demands. Unfortunately, these remembrances of their youth often times serve to criticize and not challenge, denigrate and not dignify, sabotage and not support their efforts to become responsible self- directed adults. These demoralizing and debilitating memories often emerge at the most inopportune times and become the distorted guidelines of self-defeating behaviors.

Thoreau's remembrance is our call to duty. It is a demand that we become a new voice for our kids to rely on in the years to come. Interestingly, by working diligently in the present we are preparing for the future by constructing a better past for our children to call upon when they are grown.

The Thoreau quote reminds us that the past can be brought forward at any moment and can serve as a source of resilience, comfort and strength. Recognition of this presents us the unique responsibility of becoming that voice of reason and hope that our kids will hear not only now but, perhaps more importantly, for a lifetime to come.

Love, reverence, admiration, imagination and a sense of the miraculous are elements of a nourished human spirit. All words which, when called upon by memory, are capable of transforming the present by bringing to mind the best of the past and calling into action a better self.

The power of memory allows us to become troubadours with a lifetime commission. Our words, our actions and our example play on and on, long after time, distance and circumstance have silenced our voices.

As is appropriate to this season, reflect on the year ending and picture those moments when you connected with the kids who were in your care. Be comforted! You have left an indelible image in the memories of these children, many of whom you may never see again, but in whose hearts and minds your deeds will live on until the end of time.

Disappointment

The more selfish a person the more
poignant his/her disappointments.

—Eric Hoffer

THE NEW YEAR HAS STARTED out with a disappointment. We did not advance in a grant request process despite having a very good, well thought out and well presented proposal in which many staff had a hand. It is disappointing and disheartening when things don't go our way despite our best efforts. This was no exception. Anger and depression are not too far removed from disappointment, and anger's roommate, blame, is usually not far away either.

Yet, it is probably a good time to remember how we teach our kids that attitude is a choice. No matter what happens to us, particularly if it is unpleasant or seemingly unfair, we have that option of letting it consume us by wallowing in anger, pity, depression, or blame, or we can choose to look at the situation differently. We have a choice not to become a victim of our sadness.

For instance, what can we learn from this situation? What can we do differently next time? How can we accomplish the same goal? Who else can we approach about funding our project? Are there some people who can help us approach an individual or foundation who may be willing to help?

Disappointment can become a catalyst for action and change just as much as it can destroy our hopes and aspirations. We control disappointment's destiny by making a choice to use it differently, even to a point where we may be thankful that the disappointment came our way. It forces us to look at our situation from a new perspective.

One of the false assumptions we sometimes hold is that we are *entitled to be happy*. This is especially true if we feel that we have worked hard, played by the rules, and tried to do the right thing, we should succeed. Unfortunately, that is not always the case. Sometimes, no matter how well we have prepared and how hard we have worked, the answer is still, "No." Upon receipt of the "no," the temptation presents itself to give up, stop playing by the rules, or to exact some revenge to make 'things right.' All of those paths lead, of course, to a self-destructive destination.

It takes character, as my father used to say, to get up after you're knocked down, stay the course and carry on with the work that you believe in. Disappointment is the fuel that character uses to press on.

So let us press on, always together, like Don Quixote and Sancho, "on to the next windmill." That's what we teach; that's what we must do.

Spring

PERHAPS THE SEASON MOST ASSOCIATED with hope and new beginnings, it is also a time to think about the importance of small things. These essays focus on paying attention to the detail of our lives. This attention, or lack thereof, can make an enormous difference in our life and the lives of those we serve.

Hope's duty to fill in the gaps left when faith and love fall short is highlighted in the **Stuff of Which Dreams are Made**.

The **Grace of Ease** refers to the importance of the role of teachers in our lives. It suggests that humor, role modeling and gentleness are important tools when it comes to leading others.

In the Darkest Hour is about the power of choosing one's attitude even when there is understandable cause to do otherwise.

Inspiring our kids and leading them out of the darkness caused by violence, poverty and addiction is a mission common to everyone. **Mentoring Passion** calls us to action.

Not a Moment to Lose tells a quick story about the power and necessity for forgiveness. It also emphasizes the importance of attending to the grace of the present moment.

Being ready to receive the goodness of another person's spirit at any time is the theme of **An Unexpected Debt**. The power of simplicity is touched on in this piece.

When there is ostensibly little reason to hold out hope we can take some comfort in **Statues, Stones and Flowers**. Against all odds, the weak can confound the strong.

41

We are all in this world together and more binds us than divides us. **The Tragedy in Littleton** is a quick reaction to the horrible school shooting.

Always, in concert we are more than we are alone. **Play on Together** emphasizes the beauty of teamwork.

The Stuff of which Dreams are Made

It is hard to see the future with tears in your eyes.
—Mohawk Saying

THE TOOTH FAIRY, A FREQUENT visitor to our home recently, is in good standing with my daughter, particularly because of an inflationary trend regarding tooth reimbursement. As a matter of fact, my daughter and I nearly caught the little character the other night. In case you are wondering, by my daughter's report, the tooth fairy sounds a little bit like Tinkerbelle and moves very quickly when she is flitting around the room.

The magic of believing is reflected so delightfully in my daughter's expression, I cannot but dread the day when the tooth collector's identity is made known. Even now, as she delights in anticipation of the fairy's arrival, she is pondering the logistical problems these visitations present. She is acutely aware of the high demand from the frequent visits made to her kindergarten classmates, let alone her increasing awareness of the larger world. Like so many aspects of youth, in time her belief will give way to reason. But unlike so many of the children with whom we work, her belief will be replaced by the warm acknowledge-ment that the ruse was maintained for loving purposes. Imagination,

the mother of initiative and wonder, was lovingly encouraged to have its run. Belief and faith in love will prevail and imagination, I am confident, will have a long and prosperous life within her.

In time, faith in the unseen is appropriately questioned by logic and experience. The coming of age has many connotations. Sometimes, dreadfully, this coming of age involves the premature surrender of what is commonly referred to as the 'things of youth'. In our world, where terrors both near and distant rip childish ways from children, and faith from believers in the unseen and love from the innocent, it is no wonder that hope has taken on greater importance. In fact, much of the time hope is the only thing left to fill the gap for a person whose faith has been destroyed and from whom love has been withheld.

If it is true that faith can move mountains, then hope makes the mountain first rumble. If love can conquer all obstacles in order to achieve its ends, then hope is the most potent arrow in love's quiver. Hope is the seed of ambition and innovation; it is the foundation of aspirations and desires. It is hope that sees us through the darkest hours and sustains us in our saddest moments.

Tears abate when hope rises. The Mohawk saying noted above alludes to this as it encourages us to look forward as clearly as we can. Justice prevails, but only when fueled by a hope that holds out for a better day.

The gift of hope is the most powerful legacy that we can provide to those we serve. For many children it is literally hope or nothing at all. We give them hope when we teach skills, when we role model character, when we share our kid's sorrows as well as their joys and when we help them bear their burdens.

This is the essence of our duty in caring for our kids. There is absolutely nothing more important that we can do for the children in our care. They must become, with our help, vessels of hope.

In time, bigger and stronger adult teeth will replace my daughter's lost ones. No nocturnal tooth fairy visits will be necessary in a very short while. Yet her dreams will not die. Youth's impetuous fires will soon ignite. Guided by faith and love, they will lead her to a life of passion and compassion. That is my hope for her. That is my hope for the children we serve. Hope is the stuff of which dreams are made.

The Grace of Ease

With every person who touches your heart,
Inspires a thought,
Smiles briefly in passing or for a lifetime graces your existence—
You are forever changed

—Carol Schaefer

EASING THE SPRING IS AN expression with two connotations. One is related to prepping a firearm to report and discharge a bullet. A function which, when directed towards another person, can produce instantaneous despair. Another meaning is the gradual unfolding of that season of the year most identified with new beginnings. While this piece dwells on the lessons that the season offers, the reoccurring and discouraging discharge of weapons in the halls of hope, our schools, brings these thoughts to mind. Perhaps these two connotations of *easing the spring* are linked in other ways.

My mother, having been raised on the east coast, consistently laments the lack of seasons in the deserts of Arizona. I did not fully appreciate this perennial maternal outcry until I spent some years in an area requiring a coat past ten o'clock in the morning. The drama of the seasons certainly is more easily admired when the demarcations between them are clear. In the Arizona deserts, where the distinctions among seasons are more discrete, we *ease* our way from summer to fall and winter to spring. Nature's almost imperceptible execution of *ease* is, I believe, something worth emulating in our role as teachers.

Ours is a culture that demands instant gratification and rapid solutions in most any circumstance. Our computers can't surf fast enough; our order cannot come out of the service window quickly enough. It is more than frustrating to be told that the repair of our vehicle or home will take more time than we believe we can afford. "Hurry up! Time is Money." All the while, nature whispers (teaches us), *time is life*.

Teaching, being both art and science, takes an enormous amount of time life to master. The best teachers have achieved the art of *'ease'*, that graceful mixture of imparting not only knowledge, but a way of knowing and guiding another person to want to do and be more.

The master teacher prods without pushing, encourages without excoriating and challenges without chastising. In so doing, the most powerful of all desires is triggered, the unquenchable thirst for knowledge. Most of us are fortunate if we can recall even one mentor who touched our lives in such a gentle but indelible manner, teaching us in such a way that before we knew it, spring was upon us and we wanted more.

So it is with the art of guiding our children to take effective control of their lives. The efficacy of our instruction can, in part, be measured by the *touch of ease* with which the teaching occurs. Leading by example, guiding with humor and molding by modeling are some of the *tools of ease*. The touch is also reflected in the transformation of crisis into opportunity and a restless nature that perpetually beckons, "There is teaching to be done."

The ostensibly disconnected meanings of the phrase, *easing the spring*, are linked in this fashion. The discharge of a weapon in anger or fear, leaving in its wake bewilderment and suffering, reflects the presence of an unseasoned spirit. A person in some way left untouched by the *grace of ease*. Perhaps, there is a remedy. Maybe, we need only heed the lessons of our desert seasons that gentle yet relentless teacher, that nurtures our goodness, lifts our hearts and lights our way, right before our eyes.

It is spring, I hardly noticed.

In the Darkest Hour

Everything can be taken from a person but one:
the last of the human freedoms,
to chose one's attitude in any given set of circumstances,
to choose one's own way.

—Viktor Frankl

ON MY DESK I HAVE a framed calendar page. The date on the page is February 14, 1884. The entry on the page reads, "The light has gone out of my life."

As one might infer, the author of the sentence experienced a traumatic event and is inconsolable. The author, by the way, kept a diary for nearly his entire life. His daily entry was usually pages long. This day represents the shortest entry he ever recorded.

Why, you might ask, would I keep such a depressing notation in front of me every day? The answer, I find it inspiring. That, of course, is due to the fact that I know the rest of the story.

The author, a sickly child, barely made it through his pre-teen years because of his frail condition. His father, whom he idolized and on whom he was very dependent, died when he was a young boy. Yet, he grew up to be renowned for his independence, physical stamina, incomparable intellect, and was to become, many years after this calendar entry, a symbol of persever-

ance, courage, and optimism for his generation and for those who followed. To this very day, some eighty years after his death, his name is synonymous with giving life your best shot and never giving up.

The desperate entry refers to a day when he was called back by his family to New York City. At the time of this call, he was a second year student at Harvard College. He traveled through the night from Boston and arrived in New York just in time to have his cherished mother die in his arms in the upstairs room of his boyhood home. A few hours later, his wife, in a downstairs room of the same house, gave birth to their first child, Alice. Not long after the delivery, his wife, whom he adored, passed away in his arms as a result of the complications of childbirth. In the course of a few hours, he went from gregarious and precocious student, to heartbroken son, proud father, and mourning widower. That incongruent sequence would have drained the life from many people.

The author went on to become Secretary of the Navy, Roughrider, Police Chief and Mayor of New York City, Governor of New York, Vice-President and then President of the United States, namely, Theodore Roosevelt. All of these positions achieved within one score years after the dreadful night and despondent calendar entry.

You can see then, I hope, why a disconsolate century old journal entry is such an inspiration. The message is simple. Attitude is a choice. Adversity is the mother of character, the father of courage. In the darkest hour there is hope.

Effectively, teaching our kids these lessons could bring the light back into their lives. Imagine what great teachers we would be. Imagine what our kids could become.

Mentoring Passion

Children crave a sense of self-worth. That craving is answered most readily through respectful inclusion: through a reintegration of our young into the intimate circles of family and community life. We must find ways to offer them useful functions, tailored to their evolving capacities...and embrace an ethic of sustained mentoring that extends from community to personal relationships.
Ron Powers, The Apocalypse of Adolescence,
—***The Atlantic***, *March 2002*

ENEMIES MORE FOREIGN THAN DOMESTIC have understandably monopolized our awareness these last few months. When you use passionate hatred as your primary agent of change it tends to generate violent responses from others. It remains true, to live by the sword is a dangerous, usually fatal, way of being. This is true for our kids as well.

The evil axis that preoccupies our foreign policy these days does not

overshadow the ever present tragic triad in our midst, namely, violence, poverty and substance abuse. Here in the domestic realm of our day-to-day lives we need every asset at our disposal to treat and, hopefully, prevent the countless tragedies caused when our children are caught in the relentless flailing of these thrashing scythes.

In the face of these three threshers of hopes, it is little wonder that our kids often take up the swords of anger and abuse to thrash out in self-defense. Or, as is frequently the case, turn the blade on themselves in the form of self-destructive behaviors or try to shield themselves from pain with masks of depression or delusion.

The longer you work in this world of challenging youth to take effective control of their lives, the more frequently you marvel at how kids escape this triangular scourge with the capacity to love, the thirst for knowledge and the character to say no. Yet, many do not. The alternating swirl of violence as victim or perpetrator; the frustration of not having the education to pull away from poverty; and the overwhelming temptation and snare of addiction, are powerful forces.

As guides and guardians of our kids, our task may seem self-evident. Sooth and heal, protect and nourish, teach and direct, encourage and challenge quickly come to mind. Specifically, this means providing our kids with the tools to break the cycles of violence that smother their lives, the education to escape the poverty that crushes opportunity and the self-discipline to thwart the powerful pull of substance abuse.

More is required of us. We are not only healers but builders as well. Our work demands passion. The depth and urgency of the need to intervene requires mentors who have the emotional, intellectual and moral sinew to *inspire* our children, not merely guide and guard them.

Inspire literally means to *breathe in*. It is this *breathing in* that brings love and power to our nourishing, teaching and challenging. We must demonstrate that we believe in our kids, that we are convinced of their innate goodness and capacity to overcome, learn and grow.

Our kids need power to fight back in a world where the triple threat of violence, poverty and substance abuse seem almost omnipotent. They also need love, most especially, a true mature love of self. From these reservoirs of power and love they can then draw sustenance, confidence and the courage to build a life of purpose.

The mentor who can not only teach skills but also *breathe in* passion releases their charge at the doorway of opportunity. Through that door our kids can escape from the deadly crossfire of the tragic triad and make their way to a passionate and purposeful life.

Not a Moment to Lose

*Three things in human life are important. The first is to be kind,
the second is to be kind, and the third is to be kind.*
—Henry James

She is four. She ran into the kitchen exclaiming that she needed a towel to wipe something up. Astute mom, dad, and Nana wonder aloud, "What does 'something' mean?"

'Something' is a shattered glass and water. The curiosity of a four-year-old is sometimes exposed through misfortune. Betrayed by small hands, she has inadvertently released a glass-encased dancer from the liquid confines of an ornate music box.

The panicked choice of a towel to undo the damage reveals a precocious conscience that beckons her to fix that which is broken. Her young mind has, however, underestimated the scope of damage. Her recognition of that fact is quickly exposed as she and her parents arrive simultaneously at the scene of the broken glass. The music box has played its last tune. The towel offers no solution. This calamity cannot be so easily wiped away.

Instantly, there are tears set in motion to allay primal child fears. Through moist eyes and quivering lips, all of her being is laid on the line, "Mommy, do you still love me?" An unnecessary absolution is spontaneously issued. Mother, reduced to tears that expose different fears, cradles the precious vessel of so much happiness and love. The hug does not merely forgive, it heals and rescues.

The episode took but a few moments to transpire. The emotions invoked from parents were years in the making. The impact of a loving response will portend far into the future. This crisis, as all crises do, presents the opportunity to teach. Things can be replaced, forgiveness and love play a tune that no music box can ever capture or reproduce.

Mix other ingredients into the potion of this moment and imagine the outcome. Throw in anger, guilt, recrimination, and violence, and the broken dancer becomes the precursor to a broken spirit. The broken spirit, the harbinger of so much that ails our children, demands a relentless price and extracts an enormous toll on everyone who crosses its path.

With some rare exceptions, no moment in a life scripts one's destiny for a lifetime. It is rather the cumulative effect of many such moments, as above, that brightens or deadens a future.

We, the caretakers of many broken spirits, bear the burden of those cumulative acts of violence that have beset our children. There is no towel to wipe away the pain, the terror and fear. Many hugs were missed and in their place neglect and anger expanded a void instead of filling it.

Every moment is the point of no return in the formation of a child's character. Every encounter is bursting with the opportunity to teach. Cruelty need not prevail. Kindness can overwhelm anger. Violence destroys the perpetrator and victim alike. We heal children. We have time for little else. There is not a moment to lose.

An Unexpected Debt

There is a destiny that makes us brothers; none goes his way alone:
All that we send into the lives of others comes back into our own.
—Edwin Markham

OUR EYES MET AND WE acknowledged one another with simultaneous smiles. He waved, responding to a nod. This occurred as I was pulling into a service station and he was waiting at the adjacent bus stop. Exiting the car, I had a feeling that our cryptic connection was not the end of our encounter.

Pumping gas, I had the sensation of a presence, not discerned by touch or taste, sight or hearing, or even smell. Sharing a smile had not been enough; our encounter was to be prolonged. My new acquaintance would ask more of me.

It would be fair to describe him as a disheveled, but not excessively so, thirty something year old man. An attempt had been made at combing his hair and fastening his clothes. He carried a backpack hastily put together and haphazardly placed upon his shoulders. I had a sense that he was neither the comber nor the fastener. Other hands had dressed him and sent him on his way. His presence instilled no fear and not so much empathy as pleasantness. Standing near me, a little too close perhaps for a first encounter but not disturbingly so, he spoke.

"I'm James, who are you?" Learning my name, he promptly used it in the next sentence. In other circumstances this is irritating, such as a

53

salesperson who seeks a quick and false intimacy. In this situation, it made James instantly endearing. Again, some unknown voice, much like the unknown hand that dressed him, coached him and practiced with him the rudiments of friendliness. His application of the skills was enthusiastic and innocent.

The tables had turned. Unknown to him, I was about to take more from him than he could ever want from me. The morning was still a little cool and the warmth of the sun felt refreshing. Similarly, his innocence exposed the gentleness of a person clearly not burdened by the culturally imposed complexities of life. It was a pleasure to be in the presence of one so gifted.

He stated, clearly and succinctly, the nature of the problem that called us together. A community of two, standing before a gas pump, one seeking resolution to an immediate need, one unexpectedly realizing a more deeply rooted one.

Without demand or begging he requested money for lunch. It was refreshing to meet a person who does not parse his words or calculate their impact. He was neither upset nor angry; it was as if he wanted me to share in the incredulity of how in the world he could be sent away from home with no money. He graciously accepted my meager offer to undo this injustice. What appeared to be a transaction in his favor was not. He took my money, I received his spirit.

Just then, the bus arrived. The intersection of our lives is over now, terminated with the same smile and gracious wave that began it. Smiling through teary eyes, I returned the wave. I am not sure if there is a lesson here. I only know this. There is this man named James who rides the bus. He possesses an infectious smile and a beautiful spirit. I am in his debt. I hope you meet him someday.

Statues, Stones and Flowers

To hope until love creates.
—***Percy Shelley***

AFTER ATTENDING A CONFERENCE IN Colorado on *Violence through the Lifespan*, I was left with the image of huge stones rolling down a mountainside, a rampage of unstoppable violence. I spent considerable time reflecting on the extent of, the causes for, and the comparatively meager progress we have made to reduce the pervasive plague of communal violence that infects our lives. Then I got to thinking about stones.

Michelangelo noted that he did not carve beautiful statues from stone; he merely chipped away until he uncovered the piece that had been residing in the marble all along. Although the master's self-effacement may be diffi-cult to accept, given that very few artists have been as talented at finding such beauty, the analogy of uncovering a treasure where others could only see a dull rock is compelling and life affirm-ing.

Perhaps those of us who are in the helping professions would do well to emulate this most gifted of artisans. We could do this by utilizing our resources to help our kids uncover their goodness and inner beauty instead of trying to sculpt it out of, or more accurately, on them.

While passing time in the Denver airport waiting for my flight home, I was presented with another stone parable. This time it was in the form of a poster, a flower blooming in the middle of a huge rock. The solitary flower has a striking effect because it has overcome enormous odds and yet appears so fragile against the ominous stone. The metaphors of the delicate discovered in the rough, the weak confounding the strong, the gentle taming the crude all rise. Present as well, the power of believing in something when there is no logical reason to do so.

The stone can easily represent the costume of survival that our kids often use, with layer upon layer of their protective armor comprised of the trials, travail, and tragedy of their lives. This armor, like an impregnable cloak, serves to defend a soul too frequently harmed and therefore too fragile to be exposed.

Imagine our doubting gaze upon a person who asserts that a flower would come forth to shatter such a stone, or that there could be any hope of goodness bursting through a so well defended heart. And yet, as is now self evident, a seed nestled in this very stone, soiled and tilled by a caring invisible wind, nurtured by a persistent rain, had the tenacity to prevail and thrive against all odds. The logical and experienced mind asks, is this a trick, the handiwork of some skilled florist? Is this some ruse, just another disguise of one so well defended?

Consider our *amazement* if we were a first hand witness to the flower's triumph. Consider our *dismay and surprise* when our well-chiseled diagnosis is fractured, as life asserts itself and bursts through our experienced and highbrow cynicism.

If it is true that faith can move mountains maybe it does so by cracking one stone at a time. Keeping hope alive often means retaining faith in the unseen, the unbelievable.

The danger of relying solely on our experience might be this. As adults, we know so much about stones that we no longer expect to uncover statues or encounter flowers. This profession, helping people take effective control of their lives, always needs to be refreshed. It requires that spark of youth that ignites the fire of exuberance; an exuberance that will not give up on others, no matter how thick or durable the defense, or how long the odds.

Let us be alert enough to prevent the calcification of our vision, wise enough to deter the dulling of our intuition, and hopeful enough to blunt any cynical erosion of our belief in the innate goodness and inner strength of the children and families that we serve. If the transformed stone can become the statue and the shattered rock a flowerbed, then there is always hope.

(By the way, it may be of some interest to know that the photographed flower that pierced a stone is the Official State flower of Colorado, a **columbine**.)

The Tragedy in Littleton

Not only where the rainbow glows,
But in the darkest meanest things
There always, always something sings.
—Ralph Waldo Emerson

The tragedy in Littleton, Colorado has been reverberating through the country over the last ten days. I was struck by Richard Rodriquez's, the syndicated essayist, assessment that we often fail to keep our focus on those things that unite us (i.e. stressing the importance of our communal life). While it is important for us to appreciate our differences, culturally, religiously, ethnically, our interests and orientations, we can never do so in a way that sacrifices the need to live, work, and grow together as a community.

Regardless of our differences, there is always more that unites than divides us. The shooters in this Colorado town apparently sought out those who were different, not recognizing that they were, in effect, really shooting at themselves. In some ways, it is little wonder that they ended the tragedy by abruptly and grotesquely taking their own lives.

As there is after any horrific event, there are many lessons to be learned from this tragic shooting. A very salient one may be that, while it is important to emphasize the uniqueness of our fellow students, co-workers, and clients, we can never lose sight of the fact that we are all in this struggle, to make sense of our lives, together. Clearly, our individual and group differences should serve to bring us closer together in our mutual struggle, not make it more difficult for each of us by tearing one another apart.

Left to us the living is the task of ensuring that these lives were not lost in vain. We have work to do, together.

Play on Together

Our best music is yet to be written, the strongest
and sweetest songs yet remain to be sung.
—Walt Whitman

EVERY GOOD ORCHESTRA IS COMPRISED of many talented individuals who having mastered at least one instrument, and committed to work with many

other people to create something that they could not accomplish individually on their own. Orchestras have become the classic metaphor for commitment to teamwork and to a greater good.

A finely tuned orchestra may be one of the most poignant examples of diversity creating unity. Instruments of all shapes, sizes and capabilities, interpret and express musical notes from a page in a unique way, creating beautiful sounds that can cheer, sadden, inspire, move, and motivate those who have the opportunity to listen.

Interestingly, we don't all hear the music in the same way. An overheard conversation in the lobby at intermission of an opera illustrates this point. A man, who clearly knew his music, was explaining to his companion how the horns drowned out the strings at a critical juncture in the last piece before intermission. He went on to explain how the imbalance took away from the opera singer's expression of despair at having lost her lover's affections. We both heard the same beautiful music and singing, yet he heard much more than I. A finely turned orchestra bows to an even more finely tuned ear.

There are comparisons in our day-to-day work. All of us, similar to the members of the orchestra, come together from different backgrounds, experience and education. In a sense, each bearing different instruments, to make the music that will teach, inspire, and move our kids to take effective control of their lives. And yet, no matter how well we think we have done there are, in the background, finely tuned ears, which demand that we do better, work harder, and move together more fluidly on behalf of our kids. Always, we must review our work, ensure that the horns are not drowning out the strings that our kids are able to sing on cue, and carry with them the music that we struggle so hard to teach them.

So let us play on together, knowing the music will never end. Also let us be aware that at times others must be silent while one of us plays. But most important we must remember that without helping each other, no music will be played, no lives will be changed.

Summer

The season for rest and rejuvenation, it is also a time for reflection and resolution. We do not rest for the sake of resting, but rather to prepare for days of action and daring.

Finding the meaning of your life is directly correlated to your willingness to give it away. **Summer Reflection** speaks to this concept as summer dawns instead of when it is too late.

While **Storms** is written about dealing specifically with challenging kids it also urges that we not be so risk aversive that we cannot see the opportunity that always lies in adversity.

Beyond our own walls **Always There is Work to be Done**. There really is no respite or safe haven from our duty to care for one another.

Stepping down, in order to move up, can effectively teach us many life lessons. **What's in It for Me** tries to illustrate that point.

Two individuals from the decade old Los Angeles riots still have something to teach us about working together. **Just a Thought** highlights their messages.

It seems that it is always so much easier to be critical and suspicious than it is to be open to the possibility that goodness is at play. **Assuming Good Intent** illustrates this concept.

The worst instantaneous tragedy in the lifespan of most of us occurred this fateful day. **September 11, 2001** urges a rush toward innocence.

Summer Reflection

When you leave this earth, you can take with you
nothing that you have received,
Only what you have given: a full heart enriched
by honest service, love, sacrifice and courage.

—Francis of Assisi

Francis of Assisi, a man more admired than emulated, had the presence of mind on his deathbed to rise and remove his cloak, his last possession, giving it away to the nearest person. Thus, he left the world as he had entered it, owning nothing.

There are many ways to measure one's life. We can use milestones of education, progeny, and professional status, an inventory of our accumulated assets or our net worth. However, regardless of what we approach the door of death with, we all pass through it pretty much the same. The Grim Reaper is the final equalizer. No title, connection or possession carries with it any reprieve at the end of life.

As spring yields to summer and the season of graduations and vacations approaches, it may seem a little strange to connect summer with thoughts of our last days. Yet recognition that our days are numbered encourages us to focus on the value of our most important asset, time. Thoreau said, "…the cost of a thing is the amount of what I call life which is required to be exchanged for it."

Most of us want lives connected to others, to be sprinkled with adventure, challenge and achievement. The children we serve want the same. Using Francis' criteria, this goal is tied to a life of service, love, sacrifice and courage.

Before we can live such a life we need to acquire a solid foundation in order to participate in healthy and fulfilling relationships. That foundation has a least four components we may not always recognize as important to living a full life. These components were gleaned from a speech by Dr. Warren H. Stewart, Sr. given at a conference in Phoenix, Arizona in 1998.

First, a person must be known. This means that another human being recognizes their existence as a unique individual. Kids who come into our care need to understand they are valued by virtue of their existence. It is more than knowing their name; it is knowing their story and their experience. Unconditional acceptance of others is the precursor of service to others.

Second, we all need nurturing. We all need to be cared for. The capability to love others starts with the belief that we are loveable, that someone cares.

A third, and often overlooked condition of living a full life, is the need to be needed. This is true even with the most wounded of souls. Ultimately, our own wounds can only be soothed when we are capable of soothing others. The path to maturity, of self-sacrifice for others, passes through the need to be needed. Erich Fromm noted in his book, *The Art of Loving*, that mature love can be distinguished from immature love in this way. Immature love says, "I love you because I need you." Mature love says, "I need you because I love you".

Our kids need to be inspired. They yearn to emulate and imitate a person they can admire. Courage, the virtue that allows us to practice all other virtues, is best learned by observation. It is the final element in Francis' description of a "full heart."

Maturation can be thought about as the process of developing the capacity to love and be loved. It is more than the passage from selfishness to selflessness. It is the ability to contemplate and emulate the goodness that is

to be found in our relationships. The truly inspired learn then to also cultivate goodness in others.

The soul of the self-centered is as a piece of glass with one side painted opaquely. It is like a mirror that only reflects back the narrow vision of what I want, need, and am; a looking glass with nothing beyond. While it may be a life impervious to pain, it can be a life that is devoid of passion or compassion.

The fulfilled soul is as a piece of clear glass, allowing one to both see out to and be seen by the wider world. It portends a life of vulnerability but great opportunity. It seeks to complement the hopes and dreams of others, as well as its own.

This job of challenging kids to take effective control of their lives is a daunting one, because the goal is paradoxical. We can find fulfillment in our lives by giving our life away. This is a cloudy and distant goal for those who need so much to be known, nurtured, needed and inspired so that they can have lives of service, love, sacrifice and courage.

Summer, the season of rest, is more than just a time to be refreshed. It is also a time for enriching our hearts by contemplating what we value, emulating those whom we admire and cultivating goodness in those we serve.

Storms

As we voyage along through life
'Tis the will of the soul
that decides it goal
And not the calm or the strife.

—*Ella Wheeler Wilcox*

MONSOON STORMS BRING BOTH RELIEF and danger, a break from the heat, but also menacing wind and lightening. On reflection, the storm is much like working with our kids in that the storms are inevitable, and different in the sense that our goals and that of the storms' are not the same. From the monsoon we seek shelter, with our 'kid' storms we are not so much seeking shelter from crisis, but trying to maintain our calm through it. If you have worked with kids for very long you know that it is easier said than done.

The calm we seek is a function of many things. First, of course, is our attitude, which we, unlike our troubled charges, realize is a choice we make. No one can make us think or feel or do anything that we do not choose. That concept can only be believable to you if you have skills to call upon in the middle of the storm.

Thus, the second condition of calm is mastery of the skills that you have to see you through. If a tantruming, cursing, belligerent, disrespectful, and loud child or adolescent is able to generate similar behaviors from you, clearly the most skilled person in the room is probably the kid. It takes both attitude and skill not to respond in kind. A kid's storm always has a purpose, usually has an antecedent, and has worked for him/her in the past. It is often a good cover for fear, as well as frustration and powerlessness. It takes skill to see through the disguise.

A child's storm is, more often than not, a costume of survival that typically is not removed by counter attack. Like our monsoons, it sometimes has to simply exhaust itself. The climactic storm looses its punch when it exhausts a necessary element, such as moisture, or temperature, or wind. A kid's storm winds down when it succeeds in disguising the underlying problem or when the behavior becomes dysfunctional. It becomes dysfunctional by encountering someone with the maturity and skill to teach that child that there are more effective ways to get control of his or her life.

The third condition of calm, then, is the awareness that a kid's storm is not so much a danger that needs to be avoided at all costs, but is, rather, an opportunity to teach. There are very few more pleasant aromas than the desert after a storm that has blown through. It is a great time to relax and reflect. Likewise, the aftermath of a kid's storm is often the best time to teach and gently pull away the dysfunctional costume the child has been wearing for many years. As you would expect, this is not a one-time treatment.

The fourth condition of calm is patience. You need patience to teach, review, repeat, and present in innovative ways the same information that a kid needs to hear after his fifth 'storm' on one shift. It is hard to give up a costume, especially if it has been your only line of defense for many years.

Again, the goal is not storm prevention; the monsoon can't be stopped. The objective is to provide calm in the storm and guidance after it passes.

Always, There is Work to be Done

All of life passes through the ruthless centrifuge of change.
—Carl Schorske

Summer is a time of surging energy similar to the pulsating power of the sun. The sun's perpetually exploding waves of flame can be seen and felt by us, ninety three million miles away. These rampaging infernos provide light and energy, transforming everything in their wake.

Some of us believe that it is "our great good fortune," as Holmes noted in an earlier energized time, "that while in our youth our hearts were touched with fire." Others are less than enthusiastic about the pace of life. A cosmic wave of energy seems to be carrying us towards a rendezvous with a destiny marked by continuous change. A *destiny without a specific destination* is disconcerting. It is a situation in which the most vulnerable of us are made more so.

There are many ways to measure an era. One way is to evaluate how it cares for its people. Civilized societies can be assessed not so much on how the strong and swift are doing but rather in how the weak and the slow are fairing. It is always telling when we examine how those in the *dawn* of life, the children; those at the *sunset* of life, the elderly; and those in the *shadows* of life, those unable to care for themselves, are being treated. These heliocentric times seem less brilliant under such scrutiny.

Change is the hallmark of this era. Change breeds fear in many people. Fear begets numerous maladies, the most self-defeating of which is the inclination to build walls. These walls are built almost imperceptibly, brick by brick. They are stacked to form firewalls to protect people from the blistering pace of change and exposure to those who are different. Behind these walls there is no appreciation of individual uniqueness or diversity, but rather, the insidious assertion of irreconcilable differences with others.

The individual bricks are formed by acts of commission, i.e. stark contentiousness, and by acts of omission, i.e., a benign neglect that ignores the needs of others. These bricks are bonded together with the mortar of intolerance. The resulting walls serve as a naïve and myopic assertion, "we (those of us inside the walls) are better and you (outside) are less." The walls may take many forms.

This approach to life and change has a long history of failure. Its immediate effect is to provide the illusion of a safe haven against the fiery urgencies of the day. In the extreme, the isolation generates heinous embers. These embers, when stoked by fear, periodically ignite firestorms of hatred and holocaust.

A little boy shoots a little girl in a schoolroom. We are always surprised when unrelated acts of commission and omission precipitously intertwine and spontaneously combust, yielding tragic consequences. Perhaps we shouldn't be so shocked, for always there are victims when ignorance explodes some targeted, some unintended. The unintended, more often than not, inhabit the *dawn*, the *sunset* and the *shadows* of this life.

Robert Kennedy, speaking against apartheid in South Africa, said "...*this generation can not afford to waste its substance and its hope in the struggles of the past...Beyond these walls there are lives to be saved, there is work to be done.*" Our bordered world can be bridged.

As troubadours of tolerance, we can build bridges of opportunity to serve rather than control others, particularly for those in the *dawn* of life, our children. We, the drum majors of justice, can cross those bridges and bring services to those in the *shadows*. We, the clarions of community building, can span the isolation of those in the sunset of life. *There are lives to be saved; there is work to be done.*

High walls of intolerance and bigotry cannot arrest the pace of change. Thick barriers of fear cannot prevent the need for people to work together in our ever-shrinking world. Yet, the walls will be built.

We, the teachers, we the peace builders must rise to harness the solar like energies of our times to construct, bridge by bridge, a world where the best of what is possible has a chance to come to fruition, then to endure and to thrive.

In the dawn, the sunset and in the shadows *there are lives to be saved; there is work to be done.*

What's in It for Me?

Do all the good you can
In all the ways you can
In al the places you can
At all the times you can
To all the people you can
As long as you ever can

—*John Wesley*

IF A COWORKER CALLS ON you to take a new responsibility, perhaps you should be flattered that they trusted you enough to ask. It is tempting to ask the "what's in it for me?" question. Such a request provides the opportunity to rise to the occasion and make a difference that may not only be noted by others, but bring  you the satisfaction of knowing that people trust your skills and want to give you the opportunity to develop them.

Sometimes we have to step down in order to step up. That sometimes means having to take on a disagreeable or a more intense assignment before moving on to bigger and better positions.

I can recall my eagerness to take on a higher position in a transition from being at an entry-level position in a mental health hospital. On my last shift as a technician, we had a very disturbed individual in the seclusion area. The patient chose that night to paint the entire room in his own excrement.

The evening Charge Nurse on duty was a long-time coworker who knew how eager I was to start my new position the next day. I was one of several technicians on that night, although I was probably the most senior. Despite my initial protestation that this was my last shift and I had done this many times, guess who she chose to enter the patient's room, to talk the patient down and subsequently clean up the room? She thought of it as a promotion present.

After a couple of hours of holding my breath and scrubbing the room down, I took a break and reflected on the irony of it all. Here I was prancing around thinking that things were really looking up for me and that I was somehow special and maybe a little more important than my coworkers.

To this day, I admire the wisdom of the Charge Nurse who gave me the opportunity to relearn that the most important thing to do in a crisis is respond, rise to the occasion and do what needs to be done. There was no time to ask "what's in it for me?" The question was already answered. It was a chance to be of service, to do the dirty work because I could do it well. She trusted me to handle the situation with some degree of dignity and to provide caring service to a very disturbed person.

I thanked her for teaching me to ask that question "how can I help?" instead of "what's in it for me?"

Just a Thought

I wanted you to see what real courage is. It is when you know you're licked
before you begin and you begin anyway and you see it through no matter what.
Atticus Finch from **Harper Lee's** **To Kill a Mockingbird**

Although it has become a saying that people now use as a joke, Rodney King's brief but eloquent statement during the LA riots, "Can't we all just get along?" comes to my mind this day. In a six word question he captured the essence of the need for all of us to lower our voices and listen to each other as we go about our the business of helping kids take effective control of their lives.

We seem to go through long periods of time in which we spend an inordinate amount of energy and time simply trying to do basic things, such as trying to communicate. Losing sight of our mission and vision, we labor over who is trying to do what to whom and how often.

In the past few weeks, I have heard individuals assert that:

"Administration has always had it in for our team."

"I don't know whom to trust."

"My team leader is out to get me."

"My supervisor is unprofessional, unfair, and unreasonable."

"Nobody tells me anything. I'm kept in the dark."

"I saw them looking at each other during the meeting. I know what they were thinking."

"This computer system will never work."

"There are too many changes, too fast."

"No body appreciates what I do around here."

Some of the speakers have, or are about to quit. Others suck it up because they feel stuck here, still others presumably make an attempt to deal with their concerns directly, others indirectly.

All of these concerns are perceived to be valid by the person voicing the concern. They may well be. Yet all of this is so heavy and, frankly, disheartening and wasteful of our energies. It brings to mind another player in the LA riots.

Reginald Denny, a truck driver and innocent bystander, was thrust into the national limelight during the LA riots. He was the "gentle" man who was yanked out of his vehicle and had his head crushed by repeated blows. It was not remarkable that he became a victim; he was in the wrong place at the wrong time. He had every reason to be angry, frustrated, and vengeful. His reaction, however, was remarkable. He forgave his attacker, sought no revenge, and did not assume evil intent. If there was ever a person with a legitimate beef, this was the guy. Yet, he chose a different path.

Whatever our concern, what if we take a leap of faith and assume that whatever was bothering us was not the product of bad intention or a conspiracy to do us in?   What if we assumed that our 'issue' was the product of something else, such as an oversight, or 'mis' communication, our own misunderstanding, or maybe even our own shortcomings? What if we acknowledge that dealing with our concern indirectly was not honest and therefore destructive to ourselves as well as others? What if we really did hurt somebody else, and what if we owned up to it and said we were sorry? What if we were wronged and we still forgave each other?

Pretty risky, but maybe we could get along, maybe not; just some more questions, just a thought.

Assuming Good Intent

But let this not blind you to what virtue there is; many persons strive for high ideals, and everywhere life is full of heroism.

—Desiderata

ONE OF THE MORE IRRITATING habits I have is suggesting to people that they "calm themselves down" when they are getting a bit harried or irritated at someone else or a situation. The suggestion often falls on deaf ears because the person is frequently not ready at the moment to consider the notion of having some control over how they feel.

At the risk of generating further annoyance, but hopefully a little help, let me suggest a few things to consider in order to "calm yourself down" when people or circumstances threaten to pull you down.

The Hale-Bopp comet, that traversed our skies a while back, last visited Earth 2400 years before. It will be back in about 120 generations from now. One hundred and twenty generations from now the issue that has you so hot under the collar probably won't be on too many people's minds.

Much of what we permit to get our ire up stems from an assumption that the person we are dealing with over a particular issue has "bad intent." They are trying to pull one over on us, or are trying to get us do to something we don't want or should not do. This line of thinking is, of course, self-defeating. When we assume "bad" intent, then we can't trust anything being said to us. Everything has a nuance of suspicion and subterfuge.

You may save yourself from a lot of unwarranted tension by simply assuming that the person you are dealing with has good intent, that is, they are trying to accomplish something helpful to your mutual goal of getting a particular project accomplished.

We can waste a lot of time trying to root out that monster, evil motive. The funny thing about looking for monsters is that once you start looking for them you can't stop.

The approach of assuming good intent frees us up from hunting for monsters, to look for real solutions to the problem at hand. You may often discover that the issue can be reduced to a difference in perception. The other person may simply be coming at the problem from a different point of view.

I know cynics may say to that there are people who have "bad intent" and you must therefore constantly be on your guard. That is what makes cynics such pleasant people to be around.

Yes, I know there are people, probably people we work with, who don't have good intent all of the time. I also know from experience that people who operate that way on a regular basis usually manifest their attitude many times. Usually, being in relationships with other people for very long becomes too difficult. They set up their moving on by sabotaging a relationship, quitting, or managing to get themselves fired. Of course, it wasn't their fault.

Every choice we make in every relationship reflects on what we really value. If you're complying with expectations on the outside, but always on

the lookout for the monsters on the inside of the other person, what you may really value is distrust.

When energy is directed at trying to understand the good intent of another person, you call upon what is good in yourself and the other person, even if that intent was not so good to begin with. Doing so, you demonstrate that what you really value is trust and understanding. Valuing trust and understanding will cost you something and it may be fairly painful at times.

It is also time consuming to assume good intent. This choice requires taking some risks, as well as looking at your own motives. Furthermore, you may become disheartened to discover that you might be the one who is not operating in service to others, but rather in control of others.

Sometimes what is most stressful is that we have to relinquish some degree of control over a situation in order to allow for a different perspective. This is made even more difficult if that perspective appears to be in conflict with our own values. Objectivity is rarely as simple as it sometimes is purported to be.

Difficult, as well as time consuming, is to not only discover, but admit to another person, and apologize for, your wanting to control others instead of serve them. It may be hard to accept, but it is usually more important to be kind to others in most situations than it is to demonstrate that you are right about something.

You may be thinking to yourself that this is too much to ask; too naive of an approach to others; too many people have burned you too many times? Well, you can always keep searching for the monsters of bad intent and motive. But keep in mind; you are in for a long and stressful journey. At least try to finish some time before the comet comes back!

Change

Before him he saw two roads and that terrified him –
he who had never in his life known anything but one straight line.
—Concerning Inspector Javert
From Victor Hugo's **Les Miserables**

GROWTH HAS A WAY OF challenging all of us, both organizationally and personally. It has been my experience that people who meet those challenges well are those who have a high tolerance for ambiguity, a good sense of humor, and the willingness to see change as an opportunity to learn.

I am always amused by the wide variety of responses growth evokes in people. These responses range from absolute horror to disinterested nonchalance. Certainly, there is no one right response to change. However, it does seem that what we like to think of as our best skill can get in the way of dealing with change.

For instance, people who are rigidly organized and rule driven, that is, having a mindset that has predetermined the course of things, may find change debilitating because the rules are not stable and permanent. In the play **Les Miserables**, one of the lead characters, Javert, is driven to make sure the rules are followed at any cost. He ultimately takes his own life because the incongruity of his being merciful to a rule breaker strips him of his identity. He chose to take his life rather than adapt a new view of his world.

On the other hand, people who have a more laid back approach to life are sometimes not prepared for change because they have not set up systems they can rely on in a crisis. They find themselves unable to prioritize or distinguish what is important from what is not.

I remember my father telling me that while on a ship during World War II the crew constantly drilled about what to do should the ship be attacked or catch fire. Eventually, the dreaded day came. Amazingly, out of 750 crewmembers, only one life was lost. As the ship was sinking, that crewmember went back into the ship to retrieve his false teeth. As the sections of the ship were sealed off to delay the inevitable sinking, he was trapped inside. In a crisis situation, defined as period of dramatic change, he lost sight of his priorities. He chose his teeth over his life.

The changes we go through at work are rarely as dramatic as these examples. Nevertheless, it is important for us to remember that what we may perceive to be our best asset or skill may be the very thing that is making change so difficult for us to deal with. Growth, at times, may seem painful but the alternative is always more so.

September 11, 2001

We meet under the gloom of a calamity which darkens
down over the minds of people in all civil society,
as the fearful tidings travel over sea, over land from country to country,
like the shadow of an uncalculated eclipse over the planet.
—Ralph Waldo Emerson
on the death of President Lincoln

THE EFFECTS OF THIS DAY'S TRAGIC events will reverberate for perpetuity. Our children's children will be witness to the World Trade Center's crumbling walls and the simultaneous suffocation of thousands of human lives. We will grow to envy future generations who will have the advantage of time and distance to watch those horrific video images absent the burden of trying to make sense of it in the present. Perhaps, in the broader context of history our unborn heirs will be able to critically analyze and place this event in an understandable perspective.

Now though, we are engaged in the struggle of dealing with the practical consequences of sorting through the wreckage not only of twisted metal and concrete, but also of the convolutions of psychological, philosophical and theological distress. There is no escape from this unexpected, undeserved and unwanted burden.

There is a hymn from my youth that brings some comfort to my own distress,

Stabat Mater, The Mother Stands. The piece refers to the enduring strength of a mother's love for her son as he suffers unjustly. She is powerless to prevent the injustice and has neither the resource nor the inclination to exact revenge.

It is love that brings us to life and, as we have seen and heard these last few days over and over again, love is the final concern of those who recognize their last moments on earth are upon them. All other needs, ambitions, motivations, concerns and thoughts are subservient and secondary to our need to love and be loved. In the end nothing else matters, absolutely nothing.

From the past, we should draw comfort from our Greek forbearers who advised that because of tragedy we should seek to make gentle the world. From the present, let us take solace from our preachers and poets who will bring our focus to higher purpose. From the future, let us draw an advance from the reservoir of hope that somehow because of this experience we will leave our successors a better world.

I have no other advice for a course of action, no other insight or explanation for this tragedy. Seek out and hold on to innocence wherever you can find it. Stand for love. Clearly, nothing else matters.

Autumn

While the heat begins to let up the urgencies of doing business seem to accelerate. The holidays sprinkled through the season gradually call us to community. Our connectedness is highlighted in this season of falling leaves and rising expectations.

Feeling grateful for those aspects of our lives that present particularly difficult challenges is not a common experience. **Blessings** suggest that we look on those challenges as opportunities to be thankful for.

Broadening our view of **Justice** and seeing it as a calling to break the cycle of violence is the focus of this essay. Darkness is passed from person to person until someone is willing to stand up for justice.

A long series of why questions can lead us to the importance of preparing ourselves to deal with life's most complex questions. **Why** asks us to take a look at ourselves before we venture out to help others.

Our interdependence is highlighted in **The Same Cup.** Regardless of how compelling our own mission is we can increase the likelihood of succeeding if we help others succeed at their mission as well.

Similarly, **Sawu Bona** emphasizes the importance of acknowledging others and simultaneously celebrating our uniqueness and what binds us to others.

Love demands everything, **It's a Body and Soul Job**. We must prepare ourselves for a life of passion and compassion by preparing to give everything.

Duty always beckons. **Mirrors** emphasizes the importance of taking responsibility for what occurs in your work environment.

Robert Frost eloquently exposes our desire to hold on to precious moments. **Prayers** applies his poetry to the day-to-day challenges of working with kids.

Blessings

Through many dangers, toils, and snares
I have already come;
'Tis grace hath brought me safe this far
And grace will lead me home.

—***Amazing Grace***

JONATHAN KOZOL, THE AUTHOR OF *Amazing Grace*, a book about survival in a New York City ghetto, relates that people frequently tell him how much they admire him for spending time with the poor in what they consider to be such a 'godforsaken' place. Kozol sometimes tries to explain how misplaced their admiration is and other times remains silent because he feels he cannot adequately explain that he went to the ghetto . . ."not to give blessings but to receive them."

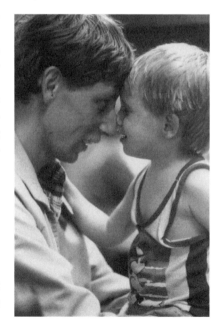

This Thanksgiving I would like to suggest that we entertain a similar notion, namely, being thankful for the opportunity to give as well as being thankful for people and things in our lives that are of importance to us. It may seem a stretch to be thankful for people who frequently test our patience, challenge our capacity to be tolerant, and wear down our resolve to be empathetic and understanding. Being thankful for people who demand much of us hardly seems to make sense.

The paradox that sometimes it takes the worst in others to bring out the best in us may also seem outlandishly incongruent. Yet, it is always in crisis that the truest self is exposed. I would suggest that our work very frequently asks us to operate in the context of a perceived crisis. It requires a strong sense of mission and resolve to be always in a giving mode.

When we think of heroics, we usually think of some outstanding or remarkable accomplishment requiring courage and acumen on the part of an individual to achieve a noble deed. We often hear the lament that there are very few heroes in our day for people to look up to or admire. I would beg to differ.

Among you, there are many heroes people who respond daily, sometimes hourly, to the challenges of working with adolescents who demand much and often give back little. The hero is the one who shows up in the 'arena' day in and day out, who knows both the heartache and exhilaration of giving oneself, . . . who explains again and again how to keep a room clean, . . . who listens repeatedly into the night about fears both real and imagined, . . . who over and over defuses anger, and does not stop caring and encouraging wounded spirits to try yet again.

I maintain that this is where and how the world is changed, one life at a time, one day at a time, one shift at a time. The job is not easy; it often demands everything of us. It's probably a hard sale, but I would also maintain that which demands much of you simultaneously blesses you. Perhaps, incredibly, I am suggesting that you also be thankful for that.

It's a Body and Soul Job

IT DEMANDS EVERYTHING

A SOUL:

that gives you strength of will
to strive, to seek, to find and not to yield
in caring for the children and families with whom you work;

that graces you with the sensitivity
to accept that it is more important to be kind
than it is to be right;

that empowers you with the knowledge that
courage and perseverance are the most important virtues.
Courage to practice all other virtues and
Perseverance to sustain your courage

A BODY:

with hearing that allows you to listen so as to understand;

with eyes to keep watch in the night so as to protect
and keep in sight that what is important is often invisible to the eye;

with a voice that can speak to console as well as to cajole;

with a heart full of compassion and passion;

with arms that wrap around to protect
and reach out to clear the way;

with gut instinct that guides you to take a chance
on a child on whom others have given up on;

with legs
to walk behind to support and care for,
to walk beside to guide and encourage,
to walk ahead to lead and challenge.

THIS IS A BODY AND SOUL JOB.

IT DEMANDS EVERYTHING.

Justice

"If a soul is left in darkness, sins will be committed.
The guilty one is not he who commits the sin, but the one who causes the
darkness."

—Victor Hugo

It strikes me that we are in the justice business. Justice is the process or act of giving back, restoring or "making it right." What is more just than our efforts to restore, to the children and adolescents we serve, the opportunity to overcome the 'darkness' that entered their lives? Darkness and violence are intertwined; one seems to beget the other.

In many respects we have been anesthetized to both the power and subtly of violence. People who watch a couple of hours of TV a day are exposed to thousands of acts of violence in the course of a year. It's difficult to make it through the front page of the paper or the first few minutes of a newscast and not be exposed to some act of senseless violence. Lost in all the publicity that violence generates is its effect on all of us, especially the kids who show up in our homes.

If justice is restoration, than injustice is the taking away of something that we are not entitled to take. When we violate a child's innocence we take away, when we hurt someone physically, emotionally, or verbally we take something away from him or her. The most serious example of course is murder, the taking away of a life. A more common example is gossip, the taking away of someone's reputation or credibility.

Closely allied with the concept of justice is that of fairness. It seems that often the principle of fairness is violated when someone ostensibly gains some advantage by acting in an unjust manner (i.e. by being deceitful, bullying, or deliberately hurtful). Generally, we would like to believe that people who behave in such a way, eventually 'get what is coming to them,' but maybe they don't. Often it's hard to see how justice is done (i.e. how restoration is made). Many times, it is indeed out of our control to bring about justice to the offender. It is not fair.

Ultimately we can only control ourselves. We can, first and foremost, make every effort not to spread 'darkness,' not to pass the bouquet of thorns that is violence. We can not undo the violence of others, but we can try to restore (i.e. bring some degree of justice) to those who have suffered through it. Often, that is our task, to carry on in spite of injustice and unfairness. We have an enormous task and responsibility, which could also be perceived as an enormous opportunity, stopping the cycle of violence and injustice. Our job is try to restore to kids for whom we work some sense that they need not be victims and that they need not victimize others to achieve justice.

We are in the justice business, shining light on the darkness.

Why?

A vision without a task is but a dream.
A task without a vision is drudgery
A vision and a task is the hope of the world.
    —From a church in Sussex, England, c. 1730

BEING THE PARENT OF A three-year-old daughter is an incredible joy. Twenty-two years ago I had been the parent of a three-year-old son. In the intervening score of years, you might think that I could easily endure a grand inquisition of one so young and inquisitive. Not true. Even now, as a more experienced parent, the fifth or sixth sequential "Why" from my daughter exhausts my entire knowledge base of information.

The challenge can come at any time and under any circumstance. The stimulus may be the reason for pouring milk on cereal or something more ethereal as in "Why is the wicky-witch so mean in the Wizard of Oz?" The result is usually the same. Dad tries to avoid complete idiocy with a "because" or "I'm not sure", or deftly tries to change the subject. All of these tricks are usually to no avail, as a three-year-old's sense of justice and need to know are absolute. There is no escape.

Let's suppose that all of us have a three-year-old willing and able to hound us during our workday. What would he or she learn about *why* we do what we do everyday?

Peter Senge, the management guru, states that 'why questions' really ask each of us to identify our *mission* in life. He goes on to say that the 'where question' asks us to identify our *vision*, as in "where are we headed?" And 'how' makes us inquire about our *values*, as in "how will we behave as we pursue our vision?"

Most agencies have a mission statement. I happen to think ours is a pretty good one. *"We build relationships that enhance the development of skills, foster a sense of worth, and embrace a belief in each child's individual potential."* It seems to answer the 'why' question, that is, why we do the work we do. It also tells people about what we value and where we hope our kids can go with our help.

While it is important that organizations have mission statements in which staff members can rally around, it is far more important for each individual have his or her own personal mission. As an old Latin proverb has it, *nemo dat quod non habet*, which literally means "nobody gives what he doesn't have." Without coherent, ethical and meaningful personal missions, we cannot give to children all that we hope to share regardless of the eloquence of the organization's mission statement.

I *wish* for you a *haunting* and a *hope*.

The Haunt: May you be haunted by the incessant whisper of duty that asks you *why you do what you do*.

The Hope: May you be inspired by your answer. May it refresh and challenge you to carry on through the fall and winter with a renewed commitment to the children in our care, many of whom are haunted by memories and experiences that have crushed their own hope.

The Same Cup

Nothing in the world in single;
All things by a law divine
In one another's being mingle

—*Percy Shelley*

ONE WAY TO THINK OF our interdependence is to compare it to a huge cup to which we all contribute and from which we all must drink. Each of us contributes to the contents of the cup through our actions and interactions. Whether the contents of the cup nourish us or poison us depends on what we, as individuals, put into it. If our contribution takes the forms of honesty, respect, kindness, loyalty, compassion, willingness to learn, and a desire to be strong for one another, then our cup's contents are very likely nourishing.

It is well to keep in mind that nourishing does not necessarily mean that the cup's contents always taste good. Being true to one's values comes with a price, and that price does not always make us comfortable. Nevertheless, we are nourished.

If our individual contribution takes the form of gossip, duplicity, intimidation, tardiness, carelessness, or dishonesty, then the content of our cup will be toxic. Inevitably, we all would be hurt.

The cup will never pass you by. You must drink from it time and time again. Your only control is to ensure that your contributions are nourishing and not toxic. Our interdependence makes it impossible to hide. Our values, hopefully, will also ensure that if someone is poisoning the cup it will not go unattended.

We cannot give what we do not have. If we don't nourish each other, the kids we serve will be the first to be affected. The agencies we serve will quickly follow.

On the other hand, if we can practice what we say we value, there is only one possible outcome, we will succeed at fulfilling our mission, namely challenging our kids to take effective control of their lives.

I urge you to ask yourself, "What is my contribution to the cup?"

Sawu Bona

What is important is invisible to the eye.
—*The Little Prince*

JUST A FEW WEEKS AGO, I attended a training in which the keynote speaker made the point that one of the most respectful actions we can take with our colleagues is to make a concerted effort to get to know them as individuals.

That may seem a rather obvious step, given that we are in the human services field. Though not intentionally we may begin relationships with others, especially our clients (kids), with false assumptions about who they are based on where they came from, their ethnicity, their education, their often turbulent family experiences, and the information passed on to us from others.

The book, *Fifth Discipline Fieldbook*, begins with the story that among the tribes of northern Natal in South Africa, the most common greeting, equivalent to "hello" in English, is the expression: **Sawu Bona**. It literally means, "**I see you.**" If you are a member of the tribe you might reply by saying **Sikhona**, "**I am here**." The order of the exchange is important; until you see me, I do not exist. The authors point out that for the tribes, it's as if when you acknowledge another person, you bring them into existence.

Similarly, we bring each other into existence, so to speak, when we take the time and the energy to get to know one another. Being culturally sensitive to you then means taking the time to listen to your individual story, in effect, the culture of you. Assuming that all people of a particular characteristic, be it religion, ethnicity, affiliation or background, think and behave in the same way is demeaning and disrespectful. '*To see you*' in the sense alluded to above is not *to see through you*, as if those obvious characteristics were of no meaning. Importantly though, it is not getting bogged down with naïve stereotypes and prejudgments about what you think and feel.

There really are no shortcuts to getting to know another person, everyone has their story and they are shaped by many personal individual experiences. Most of those experiences are unknown to us and while they maybe similar or characteristic of a particular group they are not the same for each and every individual of that group.

As much as we may like to at times, we have no right to reduce people to paper. This means that while a test score or diagnosis might give us some information about a person, it will never be the whole story. So while I may 'see you', delightfully, I will never really see or know all of you.

Mirrors

Mirror, mirror on the wall, who is responsible?

IT IS OFTEN A HARD sell, to convince people that they have some control over how they feel. It is simply easier to assign blame to the external environment, whether it be another family member, a coworker, the company, etc.

Always, we need to ask the question, "What are you doing?" If your team isn't functioning well or you dread coming to work, what are you going to contribute to fixing the problem? Are you waiting for someone else to fix it? The boss? Your immediate supervisor? Waiting for a coworker to quit or be fired?

I remember as a young boy attending a small high school, our school president standing before the student body with the topic being morale, and asking the question, "Who or what is the school?" He concluded that the school wasn't the bricks and mortar, or the curriculum, or the faculty, but we the students. I recall being taken back when he concluded that, "If the school stinks, then you stink, and the question at hand is, what are you going to do about that?"

In retrospect, that was a fairly insightful observation for a sixteen-year-old boy to make. You can rest assured that a bunch of teenage boys did not

94

want to be told, especially by a peer, that they were responsible for how they felt. "Surely the President knew what a jerk the principal was, or how lousy the food was, or how stupid some of the faculty was, or how ridiculous some of the rules were! Surely it was not our fault or our responsibility to fix anything!! For goodness sakes, we were the customers. Our parents were spending a fair amount of money to send us to this school."

Some of us continued to feel that way, and chose to be miserable for the entire year or simply quit. Others made a choice that indeed we were the "masters of our attitudes." The choice was ours, not simply to accept what we thought was wrong, but make an effort to change the things that could be changed and do our best to deal with those things that could not. The food never got any better!

As it was at that school, so I have found that in every work environment I have been confronted with the choice. The choice was to do something to change how I feel, or to wallow in being angry, frustrated, and looking for someone or something else to blame. While never particularly comfortable, I have found that the mirror always seems to reflect the picture of the guy who needs to do something.

Prayers

O hushed October morning mild
Begin the hours of this day slow.
Make the day seem to us less brief...
Release one leaf at break of day;
At noon release another leaf;
One from our trees, one far away.
Retard the sun with gentle mist;
Enchant the land with amethyst.
Slow, Slow!

—Robert Frost

The excerpt from Frost's poem, <u>October</u>, is a prayer of sorts beseeching Nature to slow the pace of autumn's transitions. The symbolism is easily imposed upon our own hectic journey as a recommendation to take a moment to reflect upon and enjoy our lives.
   O hushed October morning mild.

I am fortunate to have children whose ages span a score of years from the oldest to youngest, making me an eyewitness to life's expeditious passage. My silent, frequent and perhaps selfish prayer concerning my young daughter, "Please do not let this life pass so quickly by."
   Begin the hours of this day slow.

A similar feeling is evoked when we have occasion to gather all of our group home kids together for one event or another. Seeing all sixty or so kids at one time, I am always moved. Emotions are a mixture of anxiety and pride. Thoughts range from admiration of their resiliency to fear for their individual destinies. These children, who are more often than not products of poverty, involuntary witnesses and victims of unspeakable violence, and heirs to the misfortune of incarcerated or mentally ill parents, gather for a

moment to honor each other's presence and existence.
Make the day seem to us less brief

Their lives to this point have not offered them the option of a less-traveled road, but rather circumstance has forced them upon the pathway offering the quickest escape. This road, often passing through the child welfare system, brought them to us. From us, they head to adulthood on the highway of uncertainty and chance. More than anything, we need time; time to teach and guide, time to empower them with self-discipline, and time to show them the way.
Release one leaf at break of day.

The odds are not in their favor. A few will not even live twenty years, their lives caught and lost in the alternating swirl of violence as either victim or perpetrator or both. Some will follow their parents' footsteps to prisons and the academies of violence, there to be schooled in the arts of the underworld. Proudly, many will graduate from grade school yet never again attend another promotion ceremony in their honor, unknowingly sentencing themselves to the cycles of poverty and endless struggles. Others will become parents themselves in a very short time, growing old before they are young. But for now, there is hope. None are predestined to fail. Give us time to help them one by one.
At noon release another leaf; One from our trees, one far away.

It is easy to forget how important it is to feel safe, especially if we have managed, for the most part, to avoid the scourge of violence to our person. Unfortunately, this is often not true for most of our kids. Their energies are sometimes consumed by the self-imposed and perpetual duty of vigilance. Sometimes keeping out of harm's way is a self-defeating exercise. Hyper alert to threat, they see it everywhere. Flight, less of an option over time, devolves to fight as the only way to protect oneself. And while it may seem true that the best defense is a good offense, anger fueled by fear often has lethal consequences. So in the time we have together, we must hold sacred the need to keep our kids safe, safe from fears both real and imagined, and safe from past haunts and future uncertainties. So that they can conserve their energies to grow and learn, we must keep watch in the night.
Retard the sun with gentle mist. Enchant the land with amethyst.

Our research shows the key ingredient in the formula to lessening the long term ill-effects of early trials and trauma is time. We need time to rebuild relationships, to develop skills, to encourage and challenge and develop character and self-reliance. Time is also the foundation of trust; and trust is what all of our kids must come to have both in themselves and in those who care for them, if they are to have any chance at all.

Slow, slow.

The *October* poem, of course, asks for the impossible. Our only option is to embrace nature's cadence and use the metronome of the seasons as a guide to using our time wisely. I know clearly to cherish every hug from my daughter. Equally so, I know that not a moment with our kids can be squandered. As Frost so movingly noted in a better-known poem, we cannot rest for long

because;

The woods are lovely, dark, and deep
But I have promises to keep,
And miles to go before I sleep,
And miles to go before I sleep

About the Author

Dave Bradley

DAVE LIVES IN TUCSON, ARIZONA with his wife Debbie and daughter Brooke. He also has three grown sons, Brian, Nathan and Sean and five grandchildren. With masters degrees in education and business, Dave has been a therapist and child welfare administrator for 23 years. Currently, Dave is the Executive Director of La Paloma Family Services, Inc and is a State Representative in the Arizona Legislature.

About the Photographer
Tom Spitz

TOM SPITZ WAS BORN IN Fort Ord, California and earned a degree in Photo-Communication from California State University, Fresno in 1984. The award-winning photographer has worked for The Reno Gazette-Journal and The Orlando Sentinel, and now enjoys a freelance career covering the Southwest.

His work has been published in *The New York Times*, *The Washington Post*, *USA Today*, *Reader's Digest*, and other periodicals here and abroad. He lives in Tucson, Arizona with his wife, Jill.